The Best Career Guide for Autistic Adults 2017
Dawn Lucan

Introduction

I still remember my high school days three decades later. I remember the pressure to find the perfect career and college to attend. My high school advisor and teachers was there for me when I needed help with completing college applications. However, I was on my own when it came to deciding upon my future career.

I had some interesting challenges along the way when it came to my career since I have a disability. It made some interesting challenges when it came to dealing with some of my disability characteristics and my chosen career. However, I discovered a way to match my interests and abilities along the way.

If your chosen career requires a college degree or technical training, there is help for you out there. There is financial aid available from the government besides college scholarships. Also, the college offers a disabled students office which offers a variety of adaptations for you to be able to attend school.

The amount of resources has improved since I graduated from high school for high school students. However, it can still be a tricky matter for unique learners. I have included some of my favorite resources to help you with your new journey in life. I have created this career guide to help you find some interesting matches to your interests.

I know the job market can be frustrating at times when you are job searching. However, it is possible to find the right job for your chosen career field. At times, it may take many applications and job interviews before you obtain a job.

At other times, you may have to be creative in getting and retaining a job. In difficult economic times, jobs can be difficult to obtain and keep at times.

If you need extra income at some point with an inflexible job, you might want to consider working from home. It could be as simple as blogging or crafting. It is not much money in the beginning, but the hours are flexible since you are creating your own hours.

In this book, I often recommend for training after high school your local community college for associate's degree programs or attend the state university which is located in your specific state. I mention this, so you do not end up with a lot of debt that you could get from a private technical school or college.

I have included in this book a variety of careers that can be found in most locations in this country or the world. I have included in this book careers that require a high school diploma and in some cases a college degree.

I have included in this book variety of different website resources to help you get started in your chosen career. They include how to write a resume besides some fantastic job search that I have trusted over the years.

Dawn Lucan

Account Manager

If you love helping people and handling difficult situations, you might want to become an account manager. You could work in a variety of different industries including manufacturing, computer technology, and public relations. You would have to be great at both customer service and selling things. This is a high pressure career which does deal with commissions or receiving money after a sale. To enter into this career field, you need at least a high school diploma, but there are employers who do want you to have a college degree.

Accounts Payable Clerk

If you love math and working with money, you might want to become an accounts payable clerk. You would be dealing with invoices, paying invoices, and handling customer questions. To enter into this career field, you need at least a high school diploma, but there are some employers who want some college experience.

Administrative Assistant

If you like working in an office environment, you might want to become an administrative assistant. You could be typing correspondence, taking minutes of a meeting, arranging a business meeting, bookkeeping, and greeting visitors. To enter this career field, you need at least an associate's degree from your local community college in business.

Animal Trainer

If you love animals and want to work with them, you might want to become an animal trainer. An animal trainer works with one type of animal, but it could be a cat, dog, bird, etc. However, the most common one is a dog. You could be working in a variety of different situations including working at a retail store. To enter into this career field, you need at least a high school diploma.

Arborist

If you love plants and helping them look their best, you might want to become an arborist. You would be working outdoors in a variety of different weather conditions. You could be working for a park, a college or university, botanical garden, and utility company. To enter into this career field, you need at least a high school diploma or with some employers an associate's degree for some positions.

Assembly Technician

If you love putting things together, you might want to consider becoming an assembly technician. You could be inspecting, operating, and repairing machines. To enter into this career field, you need a high school diploma.

Baker

If you love to bake, you might want to become a baker. You could work in a bakery, retail store, restaurant, grocery, factory, or supermarket. You could be baking cookies, cakes, pies, bread, rolls, biscuits, and more each shift. To enter into this career field, you need at least a high school diploma, or you could need a certificate from a community college with some businesses.

Beauty Advisor

If you love make up and want to help women look their best, you might want to consider becoming a beauty advisor. You would be representing one vendor or make up company at a store such as a pharmacy to even a department store. You need to be experienced in customer service before they would hire you besides having great communication skills. To enter into this career field, you need to have at least a high school diploma.

Bioinformatics Specialist

If you love computers and dealing with data information, you might want to become a bioinformatics specialist. You could be working for colleges, hospitals, corporations, and government agencies. You could be working on computer databases and analyzing data. To enter into this career field, you need at least a bachelor's degree in biology along with computer courses, but there are employers out there who will require a master's degree.

Blogger

If you have passion for a subject or interest along with writing, you might want to become a blogger. It is free to start. However, it does take time in building an audience of readers. In order to make money, you do have to sign up for an affiliate program or Google Adsense. To become a blogger, you need a high school diploma or less.

Body Shop Technician

If you like working on cars, you might want to become a body shop technician. You would be working on cars that have been in an accident, and you would fix it to look like new. To enter into this career, you need to graduate from either a technical school or community college program.

Bookkeeper

If you love mathematics or working with numbers, you might be interested in becoming a bookkeeper. You would be most likely working for a small business. You would be keeping track most likely through a computer software program transaction, deposits, or number information. To enter this career field, you need at least a certificate or associate's degree from your local community college.

Brand Marketing Manager

If you love talking up a product or service you believe in, you might want to become a brand marketing manager. You would be marketing the brand from start to finish on impacting its sales. You need excellent writing and communicating skills. To enter into this career field, you need at least a bachelor's degree.

Cake Decorator

If you love to decorate and enjoy eating cake, you might want to become a cake decorator. There are people who are always searching for creative cakes for special occasions including weddings and birthday parties. You could be working for yourself, a supermarket, bakery, or grocery store. To enter into this career field, you need at least a high school diploma and a cake decorating course.

Call Center Representative

If you love talking on the telephone and helping people, you might want to become a call center representative. You could be answering questions at home or at a call center. To enter this career field, you need a high school diploma.

Case Manager

If you love helping people and great at problem solving, you might want to become a case manager. You could be working at a hospital, government agency, or nonprofit working with the disabled. You need to be great at communicating besides having the patience to deal with a lot of paperwork. To enter into this career field, you need at least an associate's degree or more in social work or human services.

Certified Nursing Assistant

If you love helping people, you might want to become a certified nursing assistant. You could be working in a nursing home, adult day care, or hospital settings. You could be helping the individual with daily life activities and lifting patients. To enter into this career field, you need to be trained for it through your local community college or hospital.

Chef

If you love to cook for yourself and others, you might want to consider becoming a chef. You could work in a restaurant, hospital, nursing home, diner, etc. Most advanced positions require college training that you can receive at your local community college.

Claims Adjuster

If you love to investigate about a situation or curious in nature, you might want to become a claims adjuster. You would be working for an insurance company investigating insurance claims in order for them to be paid. You could be inspecting buildings, motor vehicles, and more. To enter into this career field, you need at least a high school diploma, but you might need a bachelor's degree for some jobs or insurance companies.

College Instructor

If you have a passion for a particular school subject and love talking about it, you might want to become a college instructor. You can do this full or part-time depending on the college or university needs. To enter into this career field, you need at least a master's degree from a college or university, but some places do require a PhD for certain positions.

Communications Specialist

If you love writing or talking about an event or product, you might want to become a communications specialist. You could be organizing media events to promote a product or business. You could be handling advertising a product or business. To enter into this career field, you need at least a bachelor's degree from a college or university in public relations.

Computer Animator

If you love to draw and use computers, you might want to become a computer animator. You could be potentially working on video games, television programs, movies, and advertising companies. To enter into this career field, you need at least an associate's degree from your local community college, but there are companies which require a bachelor's degree.

Computer Forensics

If you love computers and investigating things, you might want a career in computer forensics. You could be working for a government agency or a corporation. You could be investing computer based crimes. To enter into this career field, you need at least a bachelor's degree and with some potential employers certification.

Computer Technician

If you love to repair things besides working on computers, you might want to consider becoming a computer technician. You could be helping people with their computers with various software and hardware issues. Most of these jobs require an associate's degree from a community college or a bachelor's degree from a college or university depending on the type of position you are looking for.

Content Writer

If you love writing and surfing the internet, you might want to become a content writer for a website. You would be writing for businesses. You could be writing for a blog or on the website. Your articles would be used to build interest in the business or product being sold. To enter into this career field, you need at least a bachelor's degree from a college or university in journalism or writing.

Crafter

If you are really creative and good with making things, you might want to become a crafter. You could work for yourself or a craft store. You could sell your craft items in a store, local craft show, or on a website. To enter into this career, you need a high school diploma or less depending on where you want to work.

Customer Service Representative

If you love helping people and problem solve, you would love to become a customer service representative. You could be helping a person over the telephone or in person at a store or business. You would need a high school diploma to enter into this field.

Database Developer

If you love working on computers and organizing information, you might want to become a database developer. You could be working in a variety of different fields such as retail (stores), government agencies, banks, colleges, and more. To enter into this career field, you need at least a bachelor's degree from a college or university.

Dental Hygienist

If you like working on your teeth and with a dentist, you might want to become a dental hygienist. You would be working in a dentist office or dental clinic. To enter this career field, you would need a certificate or an associate's degree from your local community college or technical school along with going for your dental hygienist license with your state.

Digital Media Specialist

If you love both technology and video games, you might want to become a digital media specialist. You could be working on a website, animation, or even special effects. To enter into this career field, you need at least an associate's degree from your local community college, and some potential employer's require a bachelor's degree.

Dog Walker

If you love dogs and caring for them, you might want to become a dog walker for other families. You could be setting your own hours in your own business. It does take a bit of sales experience in reaching out to potential families. To enter into this career field, you do not need your high school diploma.

Electrician

If you love to problem solve and great with tools, you might consider becoming an electrician. You could be working on residences and commercial (business) buildings. You could be working on new construction or existing buildings. To enter into this career field, you need a high school diploma, some schooling, and an apprenticeship.

Engineer

If you like solving technical problems, you might want to become an engineer. You could be working in the fields of computers, electrical, mechanical, industrial, environmental, aerospace, or civil engineering. To enter into this career field, you need at least a bachelor's degree from a college or university.

Event Marketing Specialist

If you love talking about an upcoming party or event, you might want to become an event marketing specialist. You could be working on trade shows, town fairs, concerts, sporting events, and more. You need to have good communication skills to enter into this career field. To enter into this career field, you need at least a bachelor's degree from a college or university in marketing or communications.

Financial Advisor

If you are really good at mathematics and talking up products, you might want to become a financial advisor. You could be working for yourself in business, a bank, insurance company, or other small business. You could be marketing a new financial product to a family or helping someone organize their finances. To enter into this career field, you need at least a bachelor's degree from a college or university.

Financial Analyst

If you love following the stock market and sharing your opinion on a topic, you might want to become a financial analyst. You could be working for a pension fund, bank, investment bank, securities firm, and a hedge fund. You need to have strong math and communication skills. To enter into this career field, you need to earn the Chartered Financial Analyst exam, General Securities Representative exam, and Research Analyst Exam.

Fashion Retailer

If you love clothing and helping people look their best in life, you might want to consider becoming a fashion retailer. Good qualities in a fashion retailer are a good eye for detail, negotiating, problem solving skills, teamwork, and communication skills. To enter into this career field, you need at least a high school diploma or some college experience depending on the employer and position.

Fitness Instructor

If you love to exercise or working out with fitness weights, you might want to become a fitness instructor. You could be working at a gym or fitness club. You could be working with an individual or leading a group in an exercise class. To enter into this career field, you need at least certification in fitness to work at most workplaces.

Flight Attendant

If you love to travel and fly on airplanes, you might want to consider becoming a flight attendant. You would be working for an airline that travels inside a country or abroad. You have strong skills in thinking and be able to assist others in case of an emergency. To enter into this career, you need at least a high school diploma and customer service skills experience.

Florist

If you love arranging flowers, you might want to become a florist. You could work for a supermarket, grocery store, or florist retail store. To enter into this career field, you only need a high school diploma.

Food Stager or Food Stylist

If you love taking pictures and cooking, you might want to become a food stager. You could cook the food to the right presentation point, stage it on a plate, and photograph it. You could be working for a publication, television, or large company.

Front Desk

If you like meeting people besides helping them, you might want to become a front desk person. You could be working in the hotel industry or fitness club. You need to be able to use a computer since check in is completed by a computer. Customer service is important to the position, too. To enter into this career field, you need at least a high school diploma.

Graphic Designer

If you love doing a combination of drawing and writing, you might enjoy becoming a graphic artist. You could be working on websites, company logos, print advertisements, posters, various publications, and more. Depending on the employer, you will need at least an associate's degree from a community college to enter into this career field.

Hair Stylist

If you love working with hair and a creative person, you might want to work as a hair stylist. You could be working in a hair salon or even a movie set. To enter into this career field, you need to have a cosmetology license from your state and have graduated from a beauty/cosmetology school.

Handyman

If you are great at handling various tools, you might want to consider becoming a handyman. You could be working for a company or for yourself in your own business. You could be doing construction work, painting, and simple plumbing. To enter into this career field, you need at least a high school diploma, but there are employers who want an experienced handyman.

Help Desk Specialist

If you love computers and problem solving, you might want to become a help desk specialist. You could be providing technical support over the telephone for people with software and hardware problems with their computer. To enter into this career field, you should have some background in computers or at least a certificate of completion from your local community college.

Home Health Aide

If you love helping people and want to work with people with medical problems, you might want to become a home health aide. You could be helping them around the house to various personal care. You need at least a high school diploma to enter into this career field.

Housekeeper

If you love to clean, you might want to become a housekeeper. You could be working in an office, retail store, hotel or motel, or even at someone's home. To enter into this career field, you need at least a high school diploma or less depending on your employer.

Host

If you love meeting and helping people, you might want to become a host or hostess at a restaurant or diner. You would be greeting people and seating them at a table. You would need to have great problem solving skills along with a great attitude for customer service. To enter into this career field, you would need a high school diploma.

HVAC

If you are really good at fixing and installing things including air conditioner units, you might want to become a HVAC. You could be working at homes and businesses. You could also be working on commercial refrigeration systems. To enter into this career field you need at least a certificate or associate's degree from your local community college or technical school.

Information Security Analyst

If you love computers and keeping things safe, you might want to become an Information Security Analyst. You could be working with anti-virus software, analyze security risks to the computer, investigate threats, and repair damage from security breaches. To enter into this career field, you need at least an Associate's degree from your local community college or a Bachelor's degree for some employers.

Internet Marketing

If you love talking about a product or business along with surfing the internet, you might be interested in entering the internet marketing business. You need to have strong writing and research skills. You would be focusing on search engine and social media marketing a business or product. To enter into this career field, you need at least a bachelor's degree from a college or university in communications or business.

Interpreter

Do you speak fluently more than one language? Do you enjoy helping people in life? You might want to consider becoming an interpreter. You could be helping people in a variety of different fields such as health care, tourism, legal issues, customer service, and more. To enter into this career field, you need at least an associate's degree from your local community college or a bachelor's degree depending on the employer.

Inventory Clerk

If you love organizing things and helping people, you might want to become an inventory clerk. You could be working for an individual store or as a contractor for another business. It does require some heavy lifting on a regular basis. To enter into this career field, you need at least a high school diploma.

Landscaper

If you love working outside and love plants, you might want to become a landscaper. You could be mowing the lawn, raking leaves, digging holes, trimming plants, and planting flowers, trees or bushes. These jobs are typically done at homes, businesses, and apartment complexes. I must warn you that in most parts of the country that this is a seasonal job. You need a high school diploma to start in this career field.

Librarian

If you love reading books and helping people, you might want to become a librarian. You could be working for the government, school, colleges or universities, and businesses. You could be working in a variety of different specialties such as children's, technical, legal, or general. To enter into this career field, you need to hold a master's degree in library science from a college or university.

Machinist

If you enjoy working with machines or making parts, you might want to become a machinist. You need at least a high school diploma to enter into this career field besides some vocational training through your local four year apprenticeship program, community college, or vocational school.

Manicurist

If you love nail polish and helping people look their best, you might want to become a manicurist. You could be working in a nail salon, spa, or hair salon. To enter into this career field, you need to attend cosmetology school or beauty school in addition to getting your state license.

Marketing Assistant

If you love being creative and promote a cause or project, you might be interested in becoming a marketing assistant. You need strong interpersonal and communication skills in this field. To enter into this career field, you need at least an associate's degree from your local community college or a bachelor's degree for some positions.

Market Research Analyst

If you like helping people and businesses, you might want to become a market research analyst. You would be helping a business find the best price for a particular product. You need to have strong mathematics and problem solving skills in this career field. To enter into this career field, you need at least a bachelor's degree from a college or university, and some employers want a master's degree.

Mathematician

If you love math in school and math solving problems, you might want to become a mathematician. You need to also have great communication skills besides being creative and be able to work independently. You could be working for the corporations, colleges, or the government. To enter into this career field, you need at least a bachelor's degree from a college or university.

Mechanic

If you love cars (or trucks) along with problem solving and fixing things, you might want to become a mechanic. You could work for a car (or truck) dealer, repair shop, or service station. To enter into this career field, you need to graduate from a technical (vocational) school or your community college degree along with certification.

Medical Assistant

If you love helping people and want to work in a physician's office, you might want to become a medical assistant. You could be helping in the office performing administrative duties to taking a patient's medical history. To enter into this career field, you need at least a certificate or associate degree from your community college besides certification.

Merchandiser

If you love organizing things around the house or talking about a particular topic or product, you might want to become a merchandiser. You could be educating store staff about a particular product or delivering educational materials for the store's customers. You could also be handling store inventory at times in getting rid of old stock. To enter into this career field, you need at least a high school diploma.

Music Teacher

If you love playing a musical instrument and sharing something with someone else, you might want to become a music teacher. You could be working in a variety of different settings including a college campus, music store, school, or at someone's house. You could be teaching someone how to read music or play a song on a musical instrument. To enter into this career field, you need at least a high school diploma, but you need at least a Bachelor's degree from a college or university to teach at a school.

Nanny

If you love being around children and working with them, you might want to become a nanny. You could work for a hourly, weekly, or monthly rate of pay depending on the family. You could live on your own or with the family. You could be hired directly by the family or through an agency. To enter into this career field, you need at least to have earned your high school diploma, CPR certification (optional depending on age of child), and American Red Cross first aid certification (optional depending on age of child). It does help to have some babysitting experience before applying.

Network Administrator

If you love computers and helping two or more computers communicate between each other, you might want to become a network administrator. To enter into this career field, you need at least a bachelor's degree in information systems from a college or university.

Office Manager

If you like working in an office setting doing a variety of different tasks, you might consider becoming an office manager. You could be working for a company in a variety of different industries. You could be handling mail, working on the computer, handling employees, and more depending on the company. To enter into this career field, you need at least an associate's degree from a community college to attend.

Paramedic

If you think well in an emergency and love helping people, you might want to consider becoming a paramedic. You would be traveling to an emergency situation scene and then transporting the person to the hospital. To enter into this career field, you need at least your high school diploma and post high school training to become a paramedic.

Pastry Chef

If you love to bake, you might want to become a pastry chef. You could be working at a restaurant. You could be baking cakes, pies, cookies, and more. To start in this career, you would need a high school diploma, but some businesses might want at least a certificate of completion from your local community college.

Patient Navigator

If you love helping people and the healthcare field, you might want to consider becoming a patient navigator. You need to be excellent in communication skills and organized. You could be helping people schedule appointments, working with the patient and their family, and managing health care records. To enter into this career field, you need at least a degree in social work or registered nurse from a college or university.

Pet Groomer

If you love animals and taking care of them, you might want to consider becoming a pet groomer. You could be working with cats and dogs. You could be working at a pet store, zoo, kennel, or in someone's home. To enter into this career field, you need at least a high school diploma.

Pharmacy Technician

If you love handling prescriptions, you might enjoy becoming a pharmacy technician. You could be processing prescriptions under a pharmacist, working with physician offices, and handling payments from customers. You could be working in retail pharmacy stores and hospitals. To enter into this career field, you would need in most places certification which you could find through your local community college.

Photographer

If you love taking pictures with a camera, you might want to become a photographer. You could work directly for a company or do freelance work. Some even start their own business based on their own interests. For some parts of the career field, you need at least an associate's degree in photography from your local community college. If you go into freelance work or want to own your own business, you might want to take some business courses.

Physical Therapy Assistant

If you love helping people to feel better after an accident or injury, you might want to consider becoming a physical therapy assistant. You could be working at a hospital, rehabilitative facility, nursing home, school, outpatient facility, or at a private physical therapy place. You could be helping a physical therapist with a treatment plan for a patient. To enter into this career field, you need to be certified as a physical therapy assistant.

Prep Cook

If you love to cook, you might want to become a prep cook. You could be working in a restaurant, hospital, or nursing home. You would be preparing vegetables, fruits, and various other foods for food preparation or cooking in the future. To enter this career field, you do not require any formal culinary training for most workplaces.

Product Demonstrator

If you love showing how products work and talking about them, you could become a product demonstrator. You could work in a grocery store with food or any other retail store. This is mostly part-time work, and you need a high school diploma to start in this career field.

Property Manager

If you love helping people living in a community, you might enjoy becoming a property manager. You could be working in rental community featuring apartments or townhouses. You could even manage an office building. Responsibilities include marketing, completing various paperwork, supervising repair workers, staff, answering the telephone, and more. To enter this career field, most employers prefer you to have at least a college degree from your local community college.

Public Relations

If you like communicating about a product or business, you might want to consider entering public relations. You need excellent public speaking and writing skills. You could be executing industry events and developing strategies for your product or business. To enter into this career field, you need at least a bachelor's degree in marketing or related field from a college or university.

Receptionist

If you love greeting and helping people, you would love becoming a receptionist. Besides greeting people, you would be answering the telephone and possibly some form of office work. For some positions, you might only need a high school diploma, but you could for other places need a certificate in business or office work for more advanced workplaces.

Recreation Assistant

If you love to organize and promote activities for a facility, you would love to become a recreation assistant. You could work in a nursing home, hospital, or consumer agency. To enter into this career field, you need a high school diploma to start.

Recruiter

If you like meeting people and finding the right person for the job, you might want to become a recruiter. You can specialize in a variety of different fields based on your interests. To enter into this career field, most businesses prefer you to have a bachelor's degree and some experience in human resource field.

Research Assistant

If you love science and trying to solve a scientific problem or issue, you might want to become a research assistant. You could be working for a private company or a college or university. You could be collecting data, organizing data, prepare reports, prepare articles and presentations, and handle communication. To enter into this career field, you need at least a bachelor's degree in science from a college or university.

Risk Adjustment

If you like thinking about possible scenarios about a particular situation in life, you might want to work in risk adjustment. You could be working for the government, insurance companies, and businesses. You need excellent research, customer service, and communication skills to enter into this career field. To enter into this career field, you need at least a bachelor's degree from a college or university, but there are some employers who prefer that you have a master's degree.

Security Guard

If you love helping people and monitoring situations, you might want to become a security guard. In addition, you need good communication skills and ability to handle a variety of different situations. You could have a job working for a business, hospital, educational institutions, retail stores, or even the government.-

Service Technician

If you love problem solving and fixing things, you might want to become a service technician. You need excellent customer service and writing skills. To enter into this career field, you need at least a high school diploma and in some cases vocational or technical school training with some businesses.

Social Worker

If you love working with people and helping them, you might be interested in becoming a social worker. You could work in a variety of different settings such as a nursing home, hospital, government agency, and a nonprofit organization. You could be working with patients, families, and communities. To enter into this career, you need at least a bachelor's degree in social work from a college or university along with a state license with some businesses.

Social Media Manager

If you love talking about a product besides talking on the internet, you might want to become a social media manager. You could be working on outreaching to new people, talking about the product or company, and review your strategy on a weekly basis. You need to be great at writing besides photography and videography. To enter into this career field, you need at least a bachelor's degree in marketing besides some experience with social media.

Software Tester

If you love being among the first to own a computer program, you might want to become a software tester. You would be testing a new software program before it is released for any problems or bugs contained in it. You need strong analytical (problem solving) and writing skills for this career. To enter into this career field, you need at least a bachelor's degree from a college or university.

Sports Marketer

If you love sports and talking about things, you might want to become a sports marketer. You could be working on group ticket sales, promote sponsors at events and games, handling fan entertainment, organizing group tours, and planning promotions. You could be working for a college or professional sports team. To enter into this career field, you need at least an associate's degree from a community college.

Tailor

If you love to sew and work on clothing, you might want to become a tailor. You need to have good customer service besides an eye for detail and work well with others. You could be working for a business in a store or own your own business. To enter into this career, you need at least a high school diploma or less.

Teacher Assistant

If you enjoy being around children and watching them learn, you might want to consider being a teacher assistant. You could be working at a school or daycare classroom. You could be helping with learning activities, monitoring a single child, and monitoring a group of children on the playground. To enter this career, you need at least a high school diploma, and some employers require an associate's degree from your local community college.

Technical Writer

If you love to write and great at describing technical items, you might want to become a technical writer. You could be writing instruction manuals, how to guides, journal articles, and more. You could be working in a variety of different industries. To enter into this career field, you need at least a bachelor degree in engineering, computer science, or website design.

Tour Guide

If you have a strong interest in something and expert knowledge of your area, you might want to consider becoming a tour guide. It is a person who leads a group of individuals to various sites in your area based on a theme that you have created. Most of these jobs can be located through the various bus, cruise lines, and tour companies.

Truck Driver

If you love to drive, you might want to become a truck driver. You could be traveling a local route, regional, or across the country various products for a company. To enter into this career field, you need your Commercial Driver's license or C.D.L., and you can get your training for it through a truck driving school.

Veterinary Technician

If you love animals and working with them, you might want to consider becoming a veterinary technician. At work, you would be assisting the veterinarian in treating an animal at a private clinic or veterinary hospital. To enter this career field, you need at least an associate's degree in the field.

Video Game Designer

If you love playing computer games along with telling a story and computer programming, you would enjoy becoming a video game designer. You would need a minimum of an associate's degree in software design, animation, or computer graphics from your local community college.

Video Game Tester

If you love video games and write well, you could become a video game tester. You would be playing a video game, look for problems in the video game, and then report in detail the problems to the company. To enter into this career field, you only need a high school diploma, but you need a college degree to advance in this career field.

Warehouse Worker

If you love organizing and mailing things, you might want to become a warehouse worker. You would be operating a forklift, receiving stock, storing stock in the warehouse, unloading stock from a truck, loading stock into a truck. To enter into this career field, you need to be strong because it requires heavy lifting and a high school diploma.

Welder

If you love working with metal and putting things together, you could be working as a welder. To enter into this career field, you need your high school diploma along with completing a program through your local community college or on the job training program.

Tips for Your Working Life

I know you have received many different tips from your parents, teachers, and extended family. I am going to include some tips that have helped my students over the years.

If you are attending high school or a college student, search for jobs and internships related to your future job. This will help you build your resume for your ultimate career goal.

Stay out of legal trouble when it comes to breaking the law. There are employers who run criminal background checks before hiring someone. There are employers who will not hire someone who was convicted of a crime. In addition, there are some career fields that state and federal governments that block you from entering those career fields.

Update your resume on a regular basis even if you are not looking for a job at the moment. If you have achieved a new skill or education certificate, your future employer would be interested in it. Just remember, you never know when you might be looking for a new job in the future.

Apply for jobs that you fit all of the characteristics including work availability. You are wasting your time and your potential employer's time if you do not meet all of the job qualifications for the job if you get an interview with them. This includes your work availability regarding the work schedule.

Have someone review both your resume and cover letter before submitting it. Have them check for grammar and spelling. Spelling and grammar mistakes can make a potential employer ignore your resume and hire someone else.

Be careful with your references. Check with them before you start job searching because they might not be interested in becoming one.

Dress to impress at a job interview. For men, you should wear a suit and tie. For a woman, you can wear a suit or blouse and skirt. You should not wear sneakers at all even for an interview for a job while you are attending high school.

At a job interview, never mention either your religion or disability at all. These can't be held against you at all under employment law. Employers do not look at disability, but they do look at your abilities to be able to perform the job.

Build professional relationships or friendships. They can help you locate jobs that might not be posted on the job search engines. They can also be helpful when you are job searching, and potential employers want professional references.

Take advantage of overtime when you can get it. You never know when it might end in the future. It is a great way to build your savings account.

Arrive at work on time or early for your shift. Employers keep track of your working hours. You can get into trouble if you are late too many times.

If you have a chance at a promotion at work, apply for it. You never know until you try if you will get the position. It will bring in more money for you per paycheck if you receive the promotion at work for you and your family.

Take advantage of your vacation time each year. You do not have to travel out of your area if you do not want to. You do not have to use it all at once, and you can take long weekends if you want to several times a year.

Take advantage of your company's retirement plan if they match it. I know your retirement years are many years away from now. However, you have increased retirement savings at no extra cost to you through the company matching it to a point. Remember to carry over your retirement plan into a new account if you change jobs into at a new business.

Save six months of your income in case of an emergency or job loss. The money should be placed in a savings account. You never know when you will have an emergency in life, and this money will come in handy when you need it most in life.

Working is never easy and neither is the job search. When you make the right choices in life when it comes to work and your personal life, you can impress someone enough to hire you for your dream job.

Resources

www.blogger.com
www.care.com
www.careerbuilder.com
www.careeronespot.org
www.careerperfect.com
www.createspace.com
www.dawnlucan.com
www.dawnlucansworld.com
www.dice.com
www.diversityjobs.com
www.etsy.com
fafsa.ed.gov
www.flexjobs.com
www.freelancer.com
www.indeed.com
www.monster.com
www.mrhandyman.com
www.myfuture.com
www.ncil.org
www.nerdwallet.com
www.payscale.com
www.recruitmentqueen.com
www.snagajob.com
www.technicalwriterjobs.com
www.toptal.com
www.upwork.com

Printed in Germany
by Amazon Distribution
GmbH, Leipzig